5.95

FLOWERS

THE EARTH'S GARDEN

Jason Cooper

Rourke Enterprises, Inc.
Vero Beach, Florida 32964

PHOTO CREDITS

All Photos © Lynn M. Stone

LIBRARY OF CONGRESS
Library of Congress Cataloging-in-Publication Data
Cooper, Jason, 1942-
   Flowers / by Jason Cooper.
   p. cm. — (The Earth's garden)
   Includes index.
   Summary: Introduces wildflowers, their parts, their homes
and families, and their seasonal changes.
   ISBN 0-86592-620-4
   1. Flowers—Juvenile literature.   2. Wild flowers—
Juvenile literature.   3. Plants—Juvenile literature.
4. Angiosperms—Juvenile literature.
   [1. Flowers.   2. Wild flowers.   3. Plants.   4. Angiosperms.]
I. Title.   II. Series: Cooper, Jason, 1942-   Earth's garden.
QK49.C718   1991
582.13—dc20   91-7143
                                       CIP
Printed in the USA   AC

TABLE OF CONTENTS

Flowers	5
Flower Parts	6
Insects and Flowers	9
New Flowers	11
Flower Homes	14
Flower Families	16
Wildflowers Through the Seasons	19
Garden Flowers	20
Flowers and People	22
Glossary	23
Index	24

FLOWERS

Green plants produce showy parts that we call flowers, or **blossoms.** Flower blossoms can be any color of the rainbow. They can even be the color of chocolate in some kinds of flowers.

The blossoms of grasses, bushes, and trees are flowers. But the word *flower* also refers to the many soft, green, flowering plants that are neither grasses, bushes, nor trees.

These plants, called **wildflowers** and garden flowers, include roses, lilies, triliums, tulips, orchids, and thousands of others.

Fringed gentian in a Wisconsin bog

FLOWER PARTS

A flower plant has many parts. The flower blossom itself helps the plant to make new plants. A blossom is made up of many parts, each with a special job.

Other parts of a flower plant also have special jobs. The roots anchor the plant, soak up water, and take up plant food from the ground.

The flower stem supports the blossom and transports water and food. The stem makes leaves, too. Leaves help make plant food.

The special parts of a hibiscus blossom

INSECTS AND FLOWERS

Insects, such as butterflies and bees, often visit flowers to drink **nectar.** Nectar is a sweet liquid made by the plant.

While the insect sips nectar, its body picks up tiny grains of **pollen.** As the insect—perhaps a bee—moves from one part of the blossom to another, it leaves pollen in different parts of the blossom.

Pollen grains are very important. They help make seeds from which new flower plants will sprout.

A bee with pollen grains

NEW FLOWERS

Flower seeds grow inside a berry or some other type of **fruit.** The fruit and its seeds grow on the flower stem after the flower blossom dies.

When the fruit is ripe, the seeds tumble out. If a seed finds a place to grow, a new flower plant is started.

Some flower plants live only one season. Others, like lady's slippers and irises, live for many years. Each spring their roots send up new stems, leaves, and blossoms.

A milkweed seed

White water lily in a Florida pond

Gold poppies and owl-clover in the Arizona desert

FLOWER HOMES

True wildflowers grow in almost every corner of the world. Most of them grow from soil. A few wildflowers in warm countries attach themselves to tree branches. Others, such as water lilies, grow in ponds and lakes.

Flowers live in hot, steamy jungles. They even live on cold, windy mountains where trees cannot grow. They bloom in forests, grasslands, marshes, and deserts. They grow along roadsides and in the treeless Far North.

Which kinds, or **species,** of wildflowers grow in a place depend upon the weather, soil, wind, and water.

Mountain wildflowers in Washington

FLOWER FAMILIES

Flowers in a family, or group, are not the same, but they share many of the same features. One of the biggest groups of flowers is the orchid family. This family has more than 20 thousand different species.

Different orchids look like bees, scoops, sacks, or lady's slippers. Almost all orchids, however, have remarkably small seeds and flowers with six **petals.**

Orchid blossoms may be as tiny as one-half inch across—or as large as saucers!

Yellow lady's slipper orchid in an Illinois forest

WILDFLOWERS THROUGH THE SEASONS

Each species of wildflower usually blooms once each year. Some kinds bloom in spring. Others show their blossoms in summer or fall. In warm places, such as Florida and Mexico, some wildflowers blossom during winter months.

The forest is a wonderful place to find spring wildflowers, including bloodroot and trilium. By summer, the forest is too leafy and dark for most wildflowers. Wildflowers like sunlight, and most summer and autumn wildflowers grow in open places.

Red trilium in a Connecticut forest

GARDEN FLOWERS

The first flower plants grew wild. Later, people began to take flowers from the wild and replant them around their homes.

Scientists have worked with flower seeds to make changes in the way flowers grow. Today there are hundreds of kinds of garden flowers. Some still look like their wild cousins, but many are bigger and brighter.

Some of the gardener's favorite flowers are daffodils, tulips, roses, and irises.

Garden flowers

FLOWERS AND PEOPLE

Everyone loves flowers. Many flowers are sweet-smelling as well as beautiful. The parts of some flower plants are important for use as medicines, tea, and decorations.

People raise garden flowers by planting them as seeds or small plants. Wildflowers grow freely, without any help.

Some wildflowers are hard to find. As wild places are destroyed, the flowers disappear.

A few kinds of wildflowers are rare because people have taken the plants. Wildflowers should be enjoyed where they grow best—in the wild.

Glossary

blossom (BLAH sum) — the showy bloom or flower of a plant

fruit (FROOT) — a usually soft, often tasty plant part in which seeds develop

nectar (NEK ter) — a sweet liquid made by a flower

petal (PEH tal) — the flat, leaflike structures that make up most of a flower bloom to make new flowers

pollen (PAH lin) — dustlike grains produced by flowers and necessary for flowers

species (SPEE sheez) — within a group of closely related plants, one certain kind, such as a *fringed* gentian

wildflowers (WILD flow ers) — green, soft-stemmed flowering plants that reproduce naturally in the wild

INDEX

bloodroot   19
blossoms   5, 6, 9, 11
bushes   5
Florida   19
flowers
  color of   5
  food of   6
  fruit of   11
  garden   5, 20
  homes of   14, 22
  kinds of   14
  leaves of   6, 11
  parts of   6
  petals of   16
  roots of   6, 11
  seasons of   19
  seeds of   9, 11, 16, 20, 22
  smell of   22
  stem of   6, 11

grasses   5
insects   9
irises   11
lady's slippers   11
lilies   5
Mexico   19
nectar   9
orchids   5, 16
pollen   9
roses   5
trees   5, 14
triliums   5, 19
tulips   5
water   6
water lilies   14
wildflowers   5, 14, 19, 22